The Philosophy of Benjamin Disraeli

DAVID GRAHAM

ISBN: 1503305236
ISBN-13: 978-1503305236

DISCLAIMER

All quotes within this book are in the words of Benjamin Disraeli. Although every effort has been taken to ensure the accuracy of all text, the author apologises in the event of any mistakes.

CONTENTS

INTRODUCTION

Generally regarded as one of the fathers of British politics, Benjamin Disraeli remains today one of the most influential Prime Ministers in history. Though fiercely conservative (in fact, centrally involved in the creation of the modern Conservative Party), much of his work in international affairs is still admired by people of all political persuasions.

Disraeli is notable also for his fierce rivalry with William Gladstone, the liberal politician and four-time Prime Minister. It would be an understatement to say that there was no love lost between the two.

Though born into a Jewish family, Disraeli later converted to Anglicanism at the age of twelve, following his father's dispute with his synagogue. However, although his belief in God was apparent, he is not known to have taken his religion particularly seriously.

Unlike most politicians of today, Disraeli had much of interest to say on the subject of philosophy, and was very outspoken in his views on mankind and life itself. He remains a much quoted figure today.

This book brings together some of Disraeli's most interesting thoughts on a number of different topics.

GENERAL THOUGHTS & OPINIONS

"The people of England are the most enthusiastic in the world."

*

"The pursuit of science leads only to the insoluble."

*

"There are three kinds of lies: lies, damned lies, and statistics."

*

"Nine-tenths of the existing books are nonsense and the clever books are the refutation of that nonsense."

*

"Travel teaches toleration."

*

"London is a roost for every bird."

*

"There is moderation even in excess."

*

"The more you are talked about the less powerful you are."

*

"Plagiarists, at least, have the merit of preservation."

*

"A University should be a place of light, of liberty, and of learning."

*

"Genius, when young, is divine."

*

"Change is inevitable. Change is constant."

*

"The secret of success is to be ready when your opportunity comes."

*

"Youth is the trustee of prosperity."

*

"Colonies do not cease to be colonies because they are independent."

*

"To supervise people, you must either surpass them in their accomplishments or despise them."

*

"William Gladstone has not a single redeeming defect."

*

"Almost everything that is great has been done by youth."

*

"The view of Jerusalem is the history of the world; it is more, it is the history of earth and of heaven."

*

"You can tell the strength of a nation by the women behind its men."

*

"A precedent embalms a principle."

*

"The services in wartime are fit only for desperadoes, but in peace are only fit for fools."

*

"We live in an age when to be young and to be indifferent can be no longer synonymous. We must prepare for the coming hour. The claims of the

Future are represented by suffering millions; and the Youth of a Nation are the trustees of Posterity."

*

"A great city, whose image dwells in the memory of man, is the type of some great idea. Rome represents conquest; Faith hovers over the towers of Jerusalem; and Athens embodies the pre-eminent quality of the antique world, Art."

*

"London is a modern Babylon."

*

"Assassination has never changed the history of the world."

*

"Seeing much, suffering much, and studying much, are the three pillars of learning."

*

"The Youth of a Nation are the trustees of posterity."

*

"In a progressive country change is constant; change is inevitable."

*

"If a man be gloomy let him keep to himself. No one has the right to go croaking about society, or what is worse, looking as if he stifled grief."

*

"Moderation has been called a virtue to limit the ambition of great men, and to console undistinguished people for their want of fortune and their lack of merit."

*

"There can be economy only where there is efficiency."

*

"Great countries are those that produce great people."

*

"The right honourable gentleman caught the Whigs bathing, and walked away with their clothes. He has left them in the full enjoyment of their liberal positions, and he is himself a strict conservative of their garments."

*

"An author who speaks about their own books is almost as bad as a mother who speaks about her own children."

*

"The wisdom of the wise and the experience of the ages are perpetuated by quotations."

*

"The difference between a misfortune and a calamity is this: If Gladstone fell into the Thames, it would be a misfortune. But if someone dragged him out again, that would be a calamity."

*

"There is no greater index of character so sure as the voice."

*

"Upon the education of the people of this country the fate of this country depends."

*

"Everyone likes flattery; and when you come to Royalty you should lay it on with a trowel."

HIMSELF

"Like all great travellers, I have seen more than I remember, and remember more than I have seen."

*

"My idea of an agreeable person is a person who agrees with me."

*

"I must follow the people. Am I not their leader?"

*

"I am prepared for the worst, but hope for the best."

*

"I never deny. I never contradict. I sometimes forget."

*

"I have brought myself, by long meditation, to the conviction that a human being with a settled purpose must accomplish it, and that nothing can resist a will which will stake even existence upon its fulfillment."

*

"I have been ever of opinion that revolutions are not to be evaded."

MANKIND

"We cannot learn men from books."

*

"The more extensive a man's knowledge of what has been done, the greater will be his power of knowing what to do."

*

"Youth is a blunder; Manhood a struggle, Old Age a regret."

*

"The best security for civilization is the dwelling, and upon properly appointed and becoming dwellings depends, more than anything else, the improvement of mankind."

*

"Increased means and increased leisure are the two civilizers of man."

*

"Circumstances are beyond human control, but our conduct is in our own power."

*

"Something unpleasant is coming when men are anxious to tell the truth."

*

"Nobody is forgotten when it is convenient to remember him."

*

"When a man fell into his anecdotage it was a sign for him to retire from the world."

*

"Man is made to adore and to obey: but if you will not command him, if you give him nothing to worship, he will fashion his own divinities, and find a chieftain in his own passions."

*

"Life is too short to be little. Man is never so manly as when he feels deeply, acts boldly, and expresses himself with frankness and with fervor."

*

"Taking a new step, uttering a new word, is what people fear most."

*

"Talk to a man about himself and he will listen for hours."

*

"Every man has a right to be conceited until he is successful."

*

"The health of the people is really the foundation upon which all their happiness and all their powers as a state depend."

*

"Man is only great when he acts from passion."

*

"Man is not the creature of circumstances, circumstances are the creatures of men. We are free agents, and man is more powerful than matter."

*

"You will find as you grow older that courage is the rarest of all qualities to be found in public life."

*

"As a general rule, the most successful man in life is the man who has the best information."

*

"Fame and power are the objects of all men. Even their partial fruition is gained by very few; and that, too, at the expense of social pleasure, health, conscience, life."

*

"A consistent soul believes in destiny, a capricious one in chance."

*

"One secret of success in life is for a man to be ready for his opportunity when it comes."

PHILOSOPHY

"Despair is the conclusion of fools."

*

"Desperation is sometimes as powerful an inspirer as genius."

*

"Never take anything for granted."

*

"As for our majority... one is enough."

*

"Experience is the child of thought, and thought is the child of action."

*

"The palace is not safe when the cottage is not happy."

*

"Grief is the agony of an instant; the indulgence of grief the blunder of a life."

*

"Moderation is the center wherein all philosophies, both human and divine, meet."

*

"Nurture your minds with great thoughts. To believe in the heroic makes heroes."

*

"If you're not very clever you should be conciliatory."

*

"The choicest pleasures of life lie within the ring of moderation."

*

"We are all born for love. It is the principle of existence, and its only end."

*

"The first magic of love is our ignorance that it can ever end."

*

"Justice is truth in action."

*

"I say that justice is truth in action."

*

"The fool wonders, the wise man asks."

*

"The secret of success in life is for a man to be ready for his opportunity when it comes."

*

"Action may not always bring happiness; but there is no happiness without action."

*

"There is no education like adversity."

*

"Next to knowing when to seize an opportunity, the most important thing in life is to know when to forego an advantage."

*

"Never complain and never explain."

*

"Success is the child of audacity."

*

"Mediocrity can talk, but it is for genius to observe."

*

"Duty cannot exist without faith."

*

"A majority is always better than the best repartee."

*

"Courage is fire, and bullying is smoke."

*

"Never apologize for showing feeling. When you do so, you apologize for the truth."

*

"I repeat... that all power is a trust; that we are accountable for its exercise; that from the people and for the people all springs, and all must exist."

*

"He was distinguished for ignorance; for he had only one idea, and that was wrong."

*

"Real politics are the possession and distribution of power."

*

"It destroys one's nerves to be amiable every day to the same human being."

*

"Nowadays, manners are easy and life is hard."

*

"The secret of success is constancy to purpose."

*

"What is earnest is not always true; on the contrary, error is often more earnest than truth."

*

"To be conscious that you are ignorant of the facts is a great step to knowledge."

*

"Beware of endeavoring to become a great man in a hurry. One such attempt in ten thousand may succeed. These are fearful odds."

*

"Where knowledge ends, religion begins."

*

"Without tact you can learn nothing."

*

"Time is precious, but truth is more precious than time."

*

"Frank and explicit - that is the right line to take when you wish to conceal your own mind and confuse the minds of others."

*

"Be amusing: never tell unkind stories; above all, never tell long ones."

*

"Worry - a God, invisible but omnipotent. It steals the bloom from the cheek and lightness from the pulse; it takes away the appetite, and turns the hair gray."

*

"Read no history: nothing but biography, for that is life without theory."

*

"Little things affect little minds."

*

"There is no waste of time in life like that of making explanations."

*

"We should never lose an occasion. Opportunity is more powerful even than conquerors and prophets."

*

"Every production of genius must be the production of enthusiasm."

*

"Silence is the mother of truth."

*

"Nature, like man, sometimes weeps from gladness."

*

"What we anticipate seldom occurs: but what we least expect generally happens."

*

"Diligence is the mother of good fortune."

*

"Teach us that wealth is not elegance, that profusion is not magnificence, that splendor is not beauty."

*

"Through perseverance many people win success out of what seemed destined to be certain failure."

*

"Let the fear of a danger be a spur to prevent it; he that fears not, gives advantage to the danger."

*

"Fear makes us feel our humanity."

*

"Characters do not change. Opinions alter, but characters are only developed."

*

"How much easier it is to be critical than to be correct."

*

"The greatest good you can do for another is not just to share your riches but to reveal to him his own."

*

"Adventures are to the adventurous."

*

"We moralize among ruins."

POLITICS

"Two nations between whom there is no intercourse and no sympathy; who are as ignorant of each other's habits, thoughts, and feelings, as if they were dwellers in different zones, or inhabitants of different planets. The rich and the poor."

*

"Power has only one duty - to secure the social welfare of the People."

*

"The practice of politics in the East may be defined

by one word: dissimulation."

*

"Damn your principles! Stick to your party."

*

"A Conservative Government is an organized hypocrisy."

*

"Finality is not the language of politics."

*

"The world is governed by very different personages from what is imagined by those who are not behind the scenes."

*

"In politics nothing is contemptible."

*

"Without publicity there can be no public support, and without public support every nation must decay."

*

"The very phrase 'foreign affairs' makes an Englishman convinced that I am about to treat of subjects with which he has no concern."

*

"A man may speak very well in the House of Commons, and fail very completely in the House of Lords. There are two distinct styles requisite: I intend, in the course of my career, if I have time, to give a specimen of both."

*

"Things must be done by parties, not by persons

using parties as tools."

*

"War is never a solution; it is an aggravation."

*

"No Government can be long secure without a formidable Opposition."

*

"The world is weary of statesmen whom democracy has degraded into politicians."

*

"To tax the community for the advantage of a class is not protection: it is plunder."

*

"My objection to Liberalism is this that it is the introduction into the practical business of life of the highest kind namely, politics of philosophical ideas instead of political principles."

*

"There is no act of treachery or meanness of which a political party is not capable; for in politics there is no honour."

*

"There is no gambling like politics."

*

"King Louis Philippe once said to me that he attributed the great success of the British nation in political life to their talking politics after dinner."

*

"No man is regular in his attendance at the House of Commons until he is married."

*

"Conservatism discards Prescription, shrinks from Principle, disavows Progress; having rejected all respect for antiquity, it offers no redress for the present, and makes no preparation for the future."

*

"That fatal drollery called a representative government."

*

"Nationality is the miracle of political independence; race is the principle of physical analogy."

*

"The governments of the present day have to deal not merely with other governments, with emperors, kings and ministers, but also with the secret societies which have everywhere their unscrupulous agents, and can at the last moment upset all the governments' plans."

ALSO BY DAVID GRAHAM

THE PHILOSOPHY OF MARK TWAIN

THE VERY BEST OF FRIEDRICH NIETZSCHE

www.ingramcontent.com/pod-product-compliance
Lightning Source LLC
Chambersburg PA
CBHW070502290526
45790CB00003B/1067
* 9 7 8 1 5 0 3 3 0 5 2 3 6 *